My
SPIRITUAL
JOURNEY

BY
FRANK RAMIREZ

ISBN 978-1-63814-252-2 (Paperback)
ISBN 978-1-63814-253-9 (Digital)

Covenant Books, Inc.
11661 Hwy 707
Murrells Inlet, SC 29576
www.covenantbooks.com

A Special Thank you to Donnie Tobias and Paty Ramirez for helping me write my book.

It was a hot afternoon. As a six-year-old boy who was wanting adventure and fun, I decided to climb an old tree my dad used to lift motors out of old cars with a chain that was wrapped around one of the tree's thick limbs. My dad made a living by buying old junk cars, took them home, and took them apart to sell for parts. This tree was like my dad's right hand because it helped him make a living for our family by helping him remove the motor or parts from these cars. The tree was grand and strong. Now that I think about it, this tree resembled an old, helpful, and reliable friend to my dad and myself, as I used it to experience many adventures and to escape from the world of problems, poverty, and hardships. I climbed and climbed. It seemed as if I were on top of the world when I finally reached my destination on this old friend of a mesquite tree. I recalled sitting there, grabbing on for my dear life to one of my old friend's limbs.

The view was not one that was breathtaking, but I still felt on top of the world when I was there. I could see all our neighbors' houses and yards. Many had nice, clean yards while others were struggling to mow their grass and trim their bushes. All the houses were old and in need of much repair.

Poverty was well-known in my neighborhood, but as a six-year-old boy, that was one thing I didn't worry about. I just wanted to climb, dream, and escape from the rest of the world. As I was standing and grabbing on to the tree, I felt my foot slipping. I became scared and nervous as I knew that, if I fell, I would never survive. My foot continued to slip, and the next thing I knew, I was falling off and plummeting. I could see the ground getting closer and closer. I closed my eyes. The next thing I knew, I was lying in my run-down old bed, but it felt overly comfortable, clean, and protected. I could move my legs and my arms, and I didn't have any injuries on my body. "What happened?" was the only thing I could ask myself. I could hear my mom talking to her friend in the kitchen, which was right next to my room. They were laughing and joking as if nothing had happened. Did anything happen? Did I fall off the tree? Or did someone save me from my fall? I jumped out of bed and ran to the kitchen. I asked my mom, "Mom, did I hurt myself? Did I fall off the tree?" She just laughed and said, "You're crazy, you didn't fall off any tree." After many years of thinking about my experience with my old friend, the mesquite tree, I believe I had my first supernatural experience with my higher power because I knew I was not dreaming that day and I knew I fell off that tree.

My name is Francisco Ramirez Jr. I was born on January 18, 1945, in Laredo, Texas. I was one of eight brothers and have one sister. During my life of living in Laredo, my mom, my dad, my brother, and I lived in a small house with my grandmother. During this time, my other siblings had not been born yet. I remember going one day with my grandmother to work at a restaurant where she was a waitress. I was sitting on a stool at the counter, and my grandmother placed a huge Hippo soda in front of me. I had never had a soda before. Wow, what an amazing, cold drink my grandmother had just given me. I loved her very much; she was such a hard worker, and she would express in her special way how much she loved me. I spent a lot of time with her as my mother was busy at home, taking care of my brother, cleaning the house, and making food while being pregnant with my other brother. During this time, I don't remember much about my father; however, I do remember him being a good baseball player. He had to travel during the weekends to Dilley, Pearsall, Sinton, and even Corpus Christi. He was amazing at this game, and many wanted him in their team because he was a good runner, thus making him a good base stealer. I remember seeing people jumping, yelling, and getting excited very time my dad would be on base. I wanted to play baseball just like my dad did.

After a few years, my dad decided to move our family to Pearsall, Texas. We moved to a small house next to a huge mesquite tree. The minute I jumped out of the car when we arrived at our new home, I ran straight to the tree. I looked at it and felt like a small ant next to it. I was drawn to this tree. I didn't have much interest in looking at my new room or house. I just wanted to spend time with my friend, the mesquite tree. Little did I know, this was where I was going to experience my first encounter with God.

I recall many struggles during our time in Pearsall, Texas. My dad and his brother, who also lived in Pearsall, spent a lot of time together as they would hustle to make money with junk old car parts and motors. However, he still played baseball during the weekends. My dad was very well-known in Pearsall and the surrounding towns due to his self-made business of selling parts but especially because of his skills in baseball. My dad would steal bases: second, third, and home plate. He ran fast, so shortstop was always his designated position. The bleachers were full of people, and many were there to see him play. After the game, people would want to meet him. Many times, they would even show up at our house to meet him or just talk to him. I felt like my dad was famous. Everyone wanted to see him play. Yet as a six-year-old, I never got to go see my dad play. I was too little, and my father could not take care of me and play baseball. Everything I knew about his baseball years are from stories from relatives and friends who were there to see him play. He was such a good player that teams would pay him $25 to $30 a game to play with their team. I know this doesn't seem like a lot; however, during this time of our lives, it was.

A short time later, my dad finally saved enough money to buy a piece of land for us to build a house in Dilley, Texas. So off went the Ramirez family to a new adventure of building a house. We stayed in Dilley for the rest of my childhood. Although our lives in Dilley were not those of well-off families, our lives consisted of wonderful, funny family times while growing up. When I was an eight-year-old boy, our times did not consist of playing video games or strolling down the street with a hoverboard. Our times consisted of playing outside in the hot sun with marbles. Our family would travel to San Antonio to visit my aunt on my dad's side and her family. She had a son by the name of Juan Zapata, but we called him El Chorizo. I remember him gifting me a bag full of marbles and me feeling like I had just won the lottery. I would take my bag of marbles home and played with them out in the hot sun, on the hot, burning dirt that consisted of our yard. What an amazing time my brothers and I had with this bag of marbles my cousin El Chorizo gave us. My brothers and I didn't have much, but we had one another to play and fight with.

When I was nine, my father had a new idea of becoming migrant workers. My family, my aunt's family, and my uncle's family all traveled to different parts of Michigan to pick cherries. It was hard for the entire family but well worth it because we were able to support ourselves. I would spend time with Chorizo there as we became very close. Our families worked with cherries first, then when the cherry season was over, we moved on to potatoes and then tomatoes. I also remember picking strawberries and blueberries. I don't know if we made much money as we all ate a lot of the berries while picking them. Finally, as the seasons for these fruits and vegetable came to an end, we traveled back to Texas but stopped in the state of Missouri to work on picking cotton. We would work long, hard hours.

Since I was the oldest of the boys, during our off times and the weekends, I decided to learn how to play the guitar. I had been looking for something to do since I had suffered a breakup with a girl I had fallen in love with while working there. I had met her during that time, and her parents didn't want me with her, so they took her to another city so we would not see each other. I was heartbroken and needed to find something to do that would take my mind off her. I decided to learn how to play the guitar from an old man who was working in the cottonfield alongside us. I remember learning how to play pretty quickly and the old man telling me I had an ear for music. At that time, I didn't know what that meant, but now I do.

Shortly after, as I was walking home from work, I heard the sound of someone playing the drums. When I arrived at the place we were staying, my younger brother Richard, whom we called Maruche, was playing the drums. He played as if he already knew how to play them. It was amazing. I knew he was also born with a talent for music. Shortly after, one of my cousins was selling a twelve-string guitar. I begged my dad to buy it for me, and he did since he saw that it was not only Maruche and I who were interested in music, but my other brothers were too. During the weekend, we would spend hours and hours playing our instruments and singing.

Maruche and I began to sing first. Then my brother Albert whom we called Cuyo, joined us.

At the age of sixteen, during the Christmas holiday in Dilley, I was going out to have a good time. I took a shower, put on my best outfit, and went to the town dance. As I was standing there listening to the music and watching everyone dance, I spotted a light-skinned girl out of the corner of my eye. She was the most beautiful girl I had ever seen. Her name was Gloria. I became obsessed with her, and I wanted to be with her all the time. However, her father didn't want her dating a migrant worker. According to her father, I was not suitable, nor did I make enough money for his daughter. So I decided to steal her and take her to Pearsall. Gloria and I got married, and she went to Michigan with me and my family the following year. Gloria and I had five kids: four boys and one baby girl. We were all migrants, and we enjoyed traveling and working as a family and meeting other migrant families. Many fun times were experienced, but we also experienced many illness and injuries. Still, someway, somehow, all of us always made it back home to Texas. Since my family migrated each year starting in April and we would not return till close to Christmas. I was a migrant for twenty years.

During these twenty years, in 1968, my four brothers and I decided to record an album. We didn't become instantly famous; as a matter of fact, we had to pay the recording studio for them to allow us to record the album. My brothers and I just wanted to play and sing.

It was 1969. At this point, instead of it just being my four brothers and myself, we also had one of my youngest brothers, Juan, join our band. He instantly became the main singer of our band. We called him Canchuy. At twelve years old, he got ahold of the microphone and sang with such an amazing voice. He was an instant vocalist. However, he was still a kid. When my father, who was well aware of our family's musical talent, would book us to play in little gigs like parties, weddings, or festivals, Juan did not want to go. He would hide wherever he could because he didn't want to play with the band; he wanted to play with his marbles or friends. Once, when we were fixing to leave to go play at a gig, we couldn't find Canchuy.

It was getting late, so my brother Maruche and I decided we needed to leave. As we were pulling out of the driveway, we noticed Canchuy lying flat on the roof of a small porch we had connected to our house. We stopped immediately and made him get into the truck. He cried all the way to the gig.

Our band was called Conjunto Tejano Hermanos Ramirez. During one of the many gigs my father had booked for our band, a man by the name of Ramon Montemayor heard us playing. It had not even been a week, and Mr. Montemayor had the band in a recording studio. His plan was for a major businessman who had his own recording studio from Dallas, Texas, to listen to us play. Mr. Montemayor believed so much in Los Hermanos Ramirez that he paid for us to record two songs. He was just determined for Johnny Gonzalez, the businessman from Dallas, to hear our music talent. Within another week, we were offered a contract with Johnny Gonzalez Zarape Records. This recording studio was very famous during this time. Many talented vocalists such as Agustín Ramirez, Little Joe, Ruben Ramos, and Joe Bravo were recording with them. However, the only problem Mr. Gonzalez had was our band name. He wanted us to change our name to Los Truenos de Tejas. This was a no-brainer; we had a contract! Soon after, we were on our way to Dallas to record our first official album, in which we were going to get paid. We recorded on Friday at the recording studio, and then on Saturday morning, we were recording for a TV promotion. Little did we know that that afternoon at 2:00 p.m., we were on TV! A month later, Los Truenos de Tejas was playing at Mr. Gonzalez's ballroom, El Zarape. You would think that we would be on cloud nine; however, we were just going along with what was happening. My father, on the other hand, was ecstatic. He was on cloud nine. I remember hearing him talk about his boys with such excitement in his voice. Thinking back, my brothers and I were just too young and naive to understand what had just happened to us. As always, we just wanted to play and sing.

Our first album, which had the song "Ambición" became a hit. Maruche was the singer in this song, and every radio station was playing this over and over. We were being booked left and right

8

to play at dances. During one of our gigs in Phoenix, Arizona, we played at the Calderon Ballroom. It was packed. People were everywhere, especially women. They were screaming, dancing, and trying to touch us. My brothers and I had never experienced this. We were in shock, and we knew something big was happening in our lives. People were asking for us to play the song "Ambición." We must have sung that song every thirty minutes due to so many requests. I couldn't believe how the women reacted to this song. It was as if they were falling in love with all of us. You could feel all the emotions of every person, but mostly the women in that ballroom. Our careers as musicians had begun.

At another dance back home in Pearsall, Texas, at the Wishing Well Dance Hall, we were amazed at the number of people who showed up to our event. Pearsall is a small town next to Dilley. It looked like all the population from Pearsall and Dilley was at this dance hall. I tried to see if I could remember someone from each of the towns who was not there. I could not think of one person. It was amazing to see all my family, relatives, friends, and even my enemies there.

Los Truenos de Tejas was in demand. We traveled to over twenty states. We had motor homes, buses, and station wagons in which we would travel to all these states. Vehicles would only last us a year due to the large amount of mileage they accumulated. However, with all this traveling, our wives and children stayed back home. Although our families were well taken care of financially, my brothers and I missed many important milestones in our children's lives. I wasn't there to see my first three boys' first steps. I was not there to take care of them when they were running fevers. I never took them to their first day of school. I didn't attend their football games, their birthday parties, or even their experiences of their first love or girlfriend. I even missed their graduations from high school. My first three children were basically raised by their mother while their father was traveling and playing music.

The band continued to record at least two albums per year. At first, playing at dances and festivals and traveling from one place to another was an amazing experience. The band continued to become famous and well-known everywhere we went; however, as the years passed, this life began to take a toll on all of us. Being on the road for the next ten years was not the same as what it was in the beginning. I began to realize that I was missing my family and not enjoying life with them. In addition, due to a lot of absences at home, many of our relationships with our wives suffered tremendously. Our marriages were in trouble, but our music career had to continue. We didn't know how to stop being musicians. Although the calls from home were very minimal due to my request, such call as hearing Gloria crying on the phone, telling me that our oldest son had broken his arm, was causing me to lose interest in the famous life. I recall many times when Gloria would call me. She began to tell me how she and the children were all going to church. She would beg me to go home and attend church with her. However, it was seldom that we would go home for long periods to allow us to rest and then attend family outings like going to church. Shortly after this period of my life, while in Dilley, the Lord blessed me with the opportunity to attend church with my family. I listened to the pastor with such interest. I was intrigued with the Word. I wanted to learn more. I was hooked. I enjoyed spending time with the church's members, my family, and the pastor. I had found a new interest in my life, and the music was put on the back burner. I started telling my brothers about God and church. They were intrigued too. Before we knew it, we were all attending a Christian church. I loved learning from the Bible, my pastor, and even my wife. Since Gloria began attending church before I did, she was very knowledgeable about God. Since music was all we had known, we began playing and singing Christian music instead of our old songs. My life was changing, and I didn't want to go out on the road anymore. To my surprise, my brothers were okay with it. I didn't stop completely from playing our worldly music because my brothers would ask me every so often to help them play at a gig. However, these gigs were close by and not in other states.

Still, I knew that I needed to do something to support my family. I decided to look into our migrating years and try to harvest watermelons, since Dilley was the capital of watermelons. I decided to invest in a one-ton truck in order to begin this watermelon ender during the summer, but we always continued to attend church. My two eldest boys began to help me while in the summer school break. My eldest was fifteen years old, and my second eldest was twelve. They were at the perfect age to help their father make a living for the family since my life as a musician was nonexistent during the summer. To be honest, I was just looking for another life, a better one with my family.

Summer was coming to an end, and I needed to start looking for another job to help me support my family since I didn't want to get on the road. While talking to my father-in-law, Juan Gonzalez, he began to tell me about his job as a carpenter. He had helped build many buildings in Dilley. However, during this time, Juan was suffering from gangrene on his right foot for stepping on a dirty nail. The doctors had to cut part of this leg off, and so his life as a carpenter had ended. However, little did I know that my life as one was just beginning.

Juan had spoken to me about a local real estate lady who owned many homes and needed someone to help her repair them. I decided to take my chances and go talk to her. Mrs. Asher immediately gave me a job of replacing a water heater. I had never done anything like this before. I was going back and forth, from the rent house to the local lumber and supply shop. The fittings from the water heater were causing me problems since I had never done this before. This was a totally different skill from that of a musician. I would go look at the water heater and then go look for the parts at the local shop. I was determined to master this since I knew I wanted to stay home with my family and not go out to play music with my brothers.

I took all day to figure out how to install this water heater and what I needed to install it. However, I knew that, since Mrs. Asher had been doing rental houses for many years, she knew that changing a water heater took about an hour to an hour and a half. Still, she decided to give me a chance and continued calling me for new jobs. This was the beginning of my new life, which I had been asking God for.

For the next part of my life, I was attending church, working with Mrs. Asher, and every so often, I would still go help my brothers in certain gigs if work was slow and the money was good. My faith in the Lord was growing, and although our finances weren't as good as they were when I was on the road, because my faith was increasing, I knew the Lord would take care of us all. Gloria and I began to save money. Although my job with Mrs. Asher had continued, it was during the summer while working in the watermelons and picking up a gig or two with my brothers that brought us good money to save.

During summer, we worked picking up watermelons with a local farmer named J. E. Hutchison. Soon after, the watermelon broker that was working with Mr. Hutchison asked me if I was interested in traveling to the state of Mississippi to pick up watermelons there. My eldest boys were getting older and stronger, and they had many strong friends, so I decided to make a crew of strong young boys to help me pick watermelons. I was going back to the years of being a migrant. The following year, the same broker asked me if we could also travel to Lubbock and pick watermelons there. Our summers consisted of picking watermelons in Dilley, traveling to Mississippi and Lubbock, and picking them there. Although the job was hot, long, and dirty, the money was very good. By this time, I didn't have time to play in any more gigs.

Word started spreading with the farmers about myself and my crew, and many were calling me to go work with them. For the next eight years, I began looking for strong young high school boys to join me and my boys in working on the watermelons for long, hot hours during the summer but would always go home with plenty of money. As for my relationship with God, although I couldn't attend church during the summer, I would still go during the rest of year.

But it was not all fun and games. A group of the guys I was working with started out really hardworking, but over time, they began to get really lazy and started getting into drugs. Some of my workers had trouble with money. I always prided myself on paying my workers properly. Sometimes, a worker would come up and ask for some money, so I would give them an advance from their check.

Since it was an advance from their upcoming check, their check would be a little less than it would have normally been. This went on for a while. One day, a group of workers came up and told me that they were suing me and that they wanted the money I had allegedly been shortchanging them. They had a lawyer already to go. I got a lawyer for myself, and he told me that I could win easily but that it would end up costing me more in court costs than to just pay them off now. This ultimately carried on for about a year. So I settled out of court with them.

This caused me to have a small crisis of faith. I just couldn't understand how God could let these men do and get away with something like this. During that whole sordid affair, I couldn't sleep or eat. All I could think about were the lies these men I had worked with and, indeed, even grown up with had fabricated. I still continued to play music for God and go to church. During this time, I would not be held back by anything.

Afterward, I began working with Mrs. Asher again, doing roof work. One Monday morning, we had finished doing some work. I thought about getting Jacob and Ray to go help pick up some left-over nails from the day's work, but then I reconsidered. It wasn't a lot of work, and I could easily do it myself, so I decided to let them sleep. While I was picking up the day's detritus, I heard a young girl's voice. I turned around and saw a little girl. I instantly felt sympathy for her as I took in her appearance. She was all covered in dirt, and I didn't see her mother anywhere around. I thought to myself, *She needs to get a bath!* As I was looking at her, she asked if she could help me. I responded, "No, I don't need any help!" She said again that she wanted to help, but this was no work for a three-year-old little girl. There were nails and broken bits of wood and metal all around, not the kind of place for a child. She continued to insist, so I finally told her to go ask her mother. When I started again, she came running up and said excitedly that her mother said it was okay for her to help. Exasperated, I sent her over to the clean part that I had already done the work in so she would be safe from harming herself. I was keeping an eye on her while I worked. Then I decided to ask her if she knew where Jesus was. I don't know why I asked this three-year-old if she

13

knew where he was; the words just came out of my mouth. Her response was even more surprising, however. She said yes. So I asked her where. She got up and spread her arms out toward me but was looking up above me, and she said, "He's all around you." I instantly fell to my knees, tears streaming down my face. It's like instantly all that weight from the previous year just suddenly lifted off my shoulders. I showered him with praise and thanks, for it was such a relief to know he was still there with me. From then on, I had no more worries because I knew he was with me. I never saw that girl again.

I've thought about that little girl since then, and I've come to the conclusion that it must have been God talking to me through that little girl. Why else would this little girl want to come help a stranger and say the things she did?

The next service I was in church, I told my pastor what had happened. I told him the entire story of what I had seen and heard and how I had felt. I'm not sure that he believed me then, which was unfortunate. But I suppose it didn't really matter if he believed me or not. He was a young pastor and full of youthful doubt of anything that an older gentleman like myself might say. I understand, however. How can you believe something without seeing some sort of proof?

During one of the summers, we went to pick up watermelons, a landowner from Lubbock who saw our crew at the motel across his bodega asked me if I was interested in picking up pumpkins. I refused because we didn't know anything about picking up pumpkins. The next year, we started to learn a bit more about pumpkins. We continued to work with J. E. Hutchison for another four to five years after that. When we went back to Dilley with the pumpkins and watermelons, I continued to help my brothers with playing music. We also helped Inez Asher, a local property manager, as a handyman. Whatever she needed, whether it be roofs, plumbing, painting, or other issues, we would assist her.

During this time, I began to get more involved with a Methodist church. When we went to this church, we immediately noticed the poor quality of the music, so we offered to play music for them instead. They agreed and gave us some music that we could play for them, like *corritos*. I played on my daughter's keyboard during a performance for the church. I did this because I wanted everyone to be in a good mood during the service and get closer to God. On a side note, whenever I was gone on a work trip, my daughter would play the keyboard in my absence. She also played the saxophone while I was there in the service. People were really liking the music at this time, and we noticed an uptick in popularity with the church. People were bringing their families, and the church was being recommended to their friends. The congregation of this small church boomed suddenly, bringing in people from all around. The church became so popular through our music that other churches would ask us to come and play for them, as well. I remember one time when my granddaughter, Tanya, came up and sang "Jesus, I Love You" while playing the keyboard.

The more I went to church, the closer to God I became. After I became more involved with the church, we stopped picking watermelons and focused only on pumpkins for about two months. Around this time, I told my brothers I would not be able to help them with music anymore because I was focused on helping Inez and getting closer to God.

We kept singing and continued to increase our involvement with the church.

Three years later, the pastor of our church moved out to the valley. A new pastor came to our church and quickly became unpopular due to the difference in preaching type, as compared with the old pastor, whom everyone was accustomed to. The members of the congregation who didn't like this pastor's style moved our own private service to the house of a devout member of the congregation. We began having services every Sunday. We had about five services outside. It was hot, and we had another problem. We had no pastor. We were essentially a fellowship of devout individuals getting together to talk about God.

I was starting to get fed up. As much as we wanted to have a service of our own the way we wanted it to be, it was not right to hold services without a pastor. So I stood up and said, "We're going to look for a place to have a church." They didn't really believe me. But what they didn't realize is that I was not the one who was speaking. God was talking through me.

Sometime after this, a lady named Josie came up and asked if we could play in her church on Hilltop. We agreed, of course, and set about making preparations to play for them. Elio used to help with the drums. We went to her church and played. We had the same band composition as that of before and played our hearts out for the congregation.

We played as different sets for the church. For the first set, Elio played drums, and I would play keyboard. We were the first act, or opening act, you may say. After we played, Tanya and Dominique came out, Dominique on keyboard and Tanya singing. When the service was over, it was a good service. Everyone felt closer to God. I didn't know where Tanya and Dominique were. The pastor was telling me that he could see angels dancing all around Dominique and Tanya. I didn't believe him at that time.

We had a get-together outside, where anyone was welcome. Sometime in the next week, we played at Elio's house and did the same thing. After that, I began to look for a site to build the new church. We found a building and decided this would be a good place to set up our fledgling church; however, we did not know who owned it. It was a building we used to play in and have dances. Some people I knew said that Mr. Garcia owned the building. I went and talked to him. He was a businessman, and he had no problem giving things away for a price. I asked him, "How much would the building cost?" He said that we could have it for $600. That was a bit much for us at that time, because the pumpkin-picking business had taken a turn for the worse over the last two years. I was broke at that time. My wife was not working at that time, either. The only income I had was what I got from Mrs. Asher.

About a month later, we got back into playing music. After one of these small concerts, a good friend of mine walked up to me. He was well-known in Dilley. His name was, Placido and he just handed me some money. I never asked him for money or mentioned a need for anything. The amount he gave was $600. He said he was going to give it to another church, but he decided to offer the money to me instead. Obviously, I was ecstatic. Now I could afford that building for the church.

The next day, I went to talk to Mr. Garcia. I told him I was here to buy that building from him with the $600 he asked for. He looked at me and said, "You know what, Frank? You keep that money." We came to an agreement that allowed me to use the building, but nothing came out of pocket. The only catch was that other people who paid rent to use the building would have priority and that we would need to do some minor maintenance and repairs. But still, this was clearly a blessing from God. The place was fantastic. All the chairs we could ever need were in this place.

The next day, I went to inspect the building, and I noticed one of the AC units was not functioning properly. I didn't know anything about AC, so I went to talk to Lore. He came in the next day to fix the malfunction. When he was finished, I asked him how much I owed him, and he said it didn't cost anything.

My wife and I, as well as some of the guys, started to work on the ceiling and put-up chairs. That Saturday, we were going to have a service. I asked a pastor from a neighboring town if he could come do a service for us at our church. He agreed. Brother Villarreal used to help me a lot at the church with maintenance-related issues, but most importantly, sometimes he would preach.

I started inviting everybody to be there on opening day. The church was nearly full to bursting that day. All my brothers and sisters were there, with the exception of my mother, Jacob, and his wife.

We were starting the service, and to my utter surprise, my sister arrived with my mother. The service was good. After the service, we took my mom out to eat to celebrate. It was really nice to see my mother there because she had stopped going to church.

For a time, we continued to hold services. Sometimes we would hold service with other churches, as well. On one of the services we had, my brothers were playing. Elio was seated on my left side, playing the drums. I liked the way my brothers played. It was very Christian music. Elio elbowed me to look over to my right. There was a lady dancing on the right side of the church, holding her hands up, praising God. He kept elbowing me to look over there. It wasn't anything new to me, as I have been to many, many Christian services in the past. After the third time, I stopped paying attention. While I was focused on the music, I felt something behind me to my right, like a presence. I turned around, and Elio called out, "Stop me!" I looked at him, and he was jumping up and down with his eyes wide open. He called out again, "I can't stop!" After that, he never made fun of anybody else again. I would expect not after the Holy Spirit got ahold of him.

Two to three months later, I was at home with my wife and my daughter. It was just a normal day, but I felt that God wanted to talk to me, but my wife and daughter were there. I got the feeling that he wanted to talk to me alone. At that moment, Gloria said, "Hey, you know what? Dominique and I are going to go to the store to pick up some things." They left for the store.

He clearly wanted to show me something, but I didn't know what. It's kind of hard to believe. I was there, holding my hands up. I felt a shaking, almost as if the house were moving. It was like something was coming down from above. I was scared because I did not know what was happening. I believe now that it was God. I asked, "What do you want, my God?"

He said, "Go to your bible, and point your finger somewhere on the page." The word I was pointing at ended up being an apostle. At this point, I had some doubt that I was experiencing anything. But then it was like God knew what I was feeling. He said, "Oh, you don't believe me? Turn the page, and point to another scripture." Again, I was pointing at another apostle, Peter this time, I think. I still did not believe. He told me to turn the page again, and this time, it was John. I still was in doubt, but I could see that the words I had pointed to all had meaning. But then I started to realize I had been reading this all clearly without my glasses. Normally, I would have never been able to see those words on the page without my glasses. That was when I started to believe. That was when I knew that I could have my own church. I knew everything would be okay. At this point, I cut out all my bad habits. I stopped smoking and drinking. I also promised my God that I was going to remain faithful to my wife. No more adultery.

A good friend of mine knocked on the door early in the morning, perhaps around seven. I opened the door and asked what I could do for him. He said that he wanted me to pay him what I owed. I told him I didn't owe him anything. I was confused that he was asking me for payment because I wasn't his boss and I had nothing to do with his paycheck. In a very disrespectful tone, he said again that he wanted me to pay him. I told him to not speak those words again, and then I punched him in the face. My wife and my daughter came out and gave him a towel to use for his mouth. He left and went down the stairs. A woman was waiting for him downstairs, and she said, "I told you, Buick!" Then he left.

The next Friday, I had stopped at a gas station. When I was going out of the store, the man who owed Buick and me was there. He had previously said that he would pay us Friday. I asked him what the day was, and he answered, "Friday." At that time, Buick showed up, as well. Buick apologized for acting the way he did. After that, I never had any more experiences with God.

As time moved on, my daughter and her husband moved to Corpus Christi. I continued working with the church, in addition to working at a hospital. My wife started working at a hospital, as well, for about eleven months. After that, we went to Dilley to visit some relatives. She started vomiting, so I took her to the hospital there in Dilley to see what was wrong, but she ended up being okay. I figured it would be a good idea to take her back to Corpus, so we left that same night. I decided to take her to the hospital in Corpus, as well, and they also said that she was doing fine. I took her home, but she was still vomiting profusely, so I ended up taking her back to the hospital a third time. When they checked her, they said they needed to call an ambulance so she could go to another hospital. They checked her there, and they said they needed to do an operation. We waited for about three hours, and finally, the doctor came out and said that she had a severe aneurysm.

My wife stayed in the hospital for a few months before she was released. After that, she was not the same. She was unable to take care of herself. My daughter took care of her, giving her baths, helping her walk, and feeding her. We had her in a nursing home for some time when we were unable to care of her ourselves. This went on for about eight years. Shortly after the aneurysm, my daughter separated from her husband. My daughter came to stay with me for a while, along with her kids. Dominique was working at night, so I would take care of the grandchildren during the day. Anywhere I went, I had to take the kids with me.

After some indeterminate amount of time passed, I was still helping my daughter take care of her kids. I ended up having a stroke, as well as having a hernia. I didn't go to the doctor for nearly two months because I don't really like doctors. I just didn't want to go. I ended up being in the hospital for nearly a month. After that, I told the doctors, if they didn't let me go, I was going to leave, so they ended up releasing me. I was unable to work for a while. It was a good thing my daughter was there because she took care of me, in addition to the three jobs she was working. Time passed like this for a while. My grandchildren were growing up and my daughter was, as well.

In 2013, my wife passed away due to kidney failure, and it hit us really hard. She was a huge influence in my daughter's life, so she was very much affected by the loss. She was the love of my life, and it seriously affected everyone in the family. We held a memorial for her and talked about all the things we would remember, like the fact that she was a good Christian and always came to church with me. She was a wonderful cook and would always take care of the kids when they were outside. And she always had her bible with her. I'd always have it on my mind to write about what had happened to me back in Dilley. I could never bring myself to tell anybody outright for fear of sounding crazy. I could just imagine the looks I would get! But one day, I was talking to the manager of the apartments we were staying in. I told her I was a musician. She opened up her Facebook, and I told her the name of the band. She looked it up and said, "Oh you should write a book about your life story!" So that's when I decided to write this book. Maybe a year later, I was lying on my bed, watching TV, and I heard a voice say, "Now, what is your excuse for not writing the book?"

The next day, I asked that lady if she would help me write that book. But I thought about it and later told her that I should be the one to write it. I started to write whatever I could remember from when I was younger. I started playing at church again. My cousin, Norma, had always wanted to sing with me, so I started taking her along to sing in church.

It doesn't matter if you have all the money in the world; if you don't have Jesus in your heart, you will never have fulfillment. Believe in him and stay humble for Jesus will lead us in the right direction. Love him with all your heart. Look for a good church, follow his word, and do good to others. God is real and waiting for you. Amen.

Family photo: top left to right, Ray, Tuto, Jacob,
Nandy, Dominique, Gloria and Frank

Francisco Ramirez Sr, Dominique, Eliza Ramirez.
These are the author's parents and daughter.

This was author's home in Dilley, TX where his children grew up.

Gloria and Frank Ramirez

Left to right, Frank, Jacob, Nandy, Chorizo, Tuto. Everyone gathered to help Fix up Gloria's (author's wife) grave.

Old Polaroid photo at our house in Dilley. Son
Jacob, Frank and daughter Dominique.

Gloria Ramirez (Author's wife)

Author's daughter Dominique working at a pumpkin field.

Brother Canchuy, Grandson Rene being held by Grandfather
Frank and brother Cuyo performing at a fiesta in Dilley Texas.

Daughter-in-law Rosie, oldest son Ray and Frank in Dilley.

Dominique's high school photo with her alto sax.

Frank with his granddaughters Kendra, Tanya and Tracy.

Frank's cousin Chorizo and Frank

Frank's sons Ray and Tuto

Gloria with grandkids Casey and Rene.

Son's Tuto and Nandy at pumpkin fields.

Everyone gathered before Gloria's passing. Ray,
Tuto, Jacob, Nandy, Frank and Dominique.

Gloria (wife) and Frank Ramirez

Frank, daughter Dominique and Gloria.

Author's friend Placido and Frank in Dilley.

Celebrating Frank's 66th birthday. Frank with
grandkids Casey, Rene, and Jonah.

Frank's father Francisco Sr

Frank's mother Eliza

ABOUT THE AUTHOR

Frank Ramirez was born January 18, 1945, in Laredo, Texas, to Eliza Ramirez and Francisco Ramirez Sr. He has eight brothers and one sister. Frank developed an affinity for music at a young age and began playing the guitar with his brothers. He has been playing music ever since on instruments such as guitar, accordion, keyboard, as well as providing vocals. Frank was also a migrant worker most of his life, harvesting vegetables and fruits in places such as Michigan, Colorado, Texas, and Mississippi. Frank became deeply religious during the late 1980s. Going to church every Sunday drove the Word of the Lord into him. He grew more and more interested in the Lord and eventually started becoming more involved with the church. Religion continues to be an important part of his life today, and even now, he searches for a path to the Lord in which he can praise him properly. Building a church is something he has always dreamed of and continues to aspire for in the name of God. Frank currently lives in Corpus Christi, Texas, and works as a handyman.

Frank is a very caring person and will do anything for his family and friends. He married his wife at a very young age and loved her very much. As with any marriage, there were hardships, but they both stuck it out together. This book is something he has wanted to write for a very long time, and he is ecstatic about the chance to have his experiences lived by someone else.